THE FLORIDA KEYS
PORTS OF CALL & ANCHORAGES

By THOMAS A. HENSCHEL
Aerial Photography by JOSEPH R. MELANSON

Caeser Creek, Biscayne Bay

PUBLISHED BY

Mile High Publishing & Graphics
217 Paragon Parkway • #112
Clyde, NC 28721-8509
Tel. & Fax: 828-627-9104
Toll Free: 1-888-818-6640
Web Site: www.cruisingbook.com
E-Mail: info@cruisingbook.com

DISTRIBUTED BY

Cruising Guide Publications
P.O. Box 1017
Dunedin, Florida 34697-1017
Phone: (800) 330-9542 • (727) 733-5322
Fax: • (727) 734-8179
Web Site: www.cruisingguides.com • E-Mail: info@cruisingguides.com

By THOMAS A. HENSCHEL
Publisher

AERIAL PHOTOGRAPHY
Joseph R. Melanson

ASSOCIATE PUBLISHER
Lee Marie Pischedda

EDITOR
Janey Franklin

EDITORIAL CONSULTANT
Harlan Franklin

DESIGN & GRAPHICS
Thomas A. Henschel

ON THE COVER
Indian Key Channel, Indian Key and Lignumvitae Key
Snorkeling in the Keys photo by Stephen Frink, Key Largo, FL

DEDICATION
To Lee Whitney Young... a fellow reader and traveler.
"All roads are open to those that have the will to travel." -- tah

The "Sandbar" on a weekend at Whale Harbor Channel.

The Cape Florida lighthouse at Bill Baggs Cape Florida State Park on Key Biscayne.

CONTENTS

Introduction 9
Fishing The Keys by Harlan Franklin 13
Beneath The Seas 15
BISCAYNE BAY
Government Cut, Miami 20
Virginia Key 22
Key Biscayne, Crandon Park Marina 24
Key Biscayne, Cape Florida 26
Dinner Key & Coconut Grove 28
Elliott Key, Biscayne Bay 30
UPPER KEYS
Little Card Sound, Barnes Sound & Card Sound Bridge 32
Jewfish Creek 34
Dusenbury Creek, Grouper Creek & Marvin D. Adams Waterway 36
Key Largo & Largo Sound 38
Tavernier Community Harbor & Mangrove Marina 40
Tavernier Creek 42
Plantation Yacht Harbor 44
Snake Creek 46

Whale Harbor Channel 48
MIDDLE KEYS
Little Basin, World Wide Sportsman Bayside Marina 50
Upper Matecumbe Key, Bud N' Mary's Marina 52
Indian Key Channel 54
Lower Matecumbe Key, Caloosa Cove Marina 56
Hawk's Cay Resort & Marina 58
Key Colony Beach 60
Boot Key Harbor, Marathon 62
Faro Blanco Resort & Marina 64
LOWER KEYS
Sunshine & Bahia Honda Keys 66
Newfound Harbor Channel & Little Palm Island Resort 68
Stock Island & Oceanside Marina 70
Key West 72
Key West Bight & Historic Seaport 74
Boca Grande & Marquesas Keys 76
Dry Tortugas & Fort Jefferson 78

The Lorelei Restaurant, Cabana Bar and Marina at Upper Matecumbe Key.

Boca Chita Key, Biscayne Bay

Sunsets are a cause for celebration in the Keys. A sportfishing boat sets out for bluewater fishing and wading the flats on the opposite page.
Photos Visit Florida

INTRODUCTION

by Thomas A. Henschel

The Florida Keys represent a magical destination for the cruising boater, sportfisherman or the watersports enthusiast. The magic for the cruising boater includes countless attractive anchorages and a wealth of modern marinas in a wide variety of destinations. The Keys offer the worlds' finest fishing and diving or snorkeling over the coral reefs that can only be described as spectacular.

This book highlights many of the Keys ports of call and anchorages, and it is not meant to be a guide, but rather used in conjunction along with other fine boating guides published about the Keys and recommended navigation charts. While Biscayne Bay and portions of Miami may not be technically part of the "real" Keys, they have been included since they are important stepping off points for the island paradise found to the south.

THE UPPER KEYS

Key Largo is known as the diving capital of the world and the showcase of this island lies just offshore, the John Pennekamp State Park which is the first underwater preserve in the country. Here divers and snorkelers will have the opportunity to view more than 600 species of tropical fish and a wide variety of types of coral. At the park, which is part of the Florida Keys National Marine Sanctuary, visitors can take part in canoe trips, picnicking, camping, fishing, boating and many other activities. A state operated marina is also part of the park.

Key Largo is a sprawling region comprised of strip malls, dive centers, colorful shops and numerous marinas. For the most part, most of these marinas cater to smaller craft and dockage for cruising vessels is somewhat limited. The exception is the Rock Harbor section on the ocean where there are several fine marinas. Here you will also find the original *African Queen*, made famous by Humphrey Bogart and Katherine Hepburn in the movie of the same name.

Farther down Key Largo is the small community of Tavernier. Reportedly, this town was named by the sailors who visited there in bygone years and found plenty of taverns where they could quench their thirst after voyages. The town remains interesting as many of the turn-of-the-century homes have been restored.

Continued on Page 10

Sombrero Reef light off Marathon in the Atlantic Ocean is a popular diving and snorkeling site.

A Key deer on Big Pine Key. Photo Tom Henschel

Continued from Page 9

The upper Keys with its wide spectrum of watersports activities, shopping and attractions remains one of the most popular places to visit in the country.

MIDDLE KEYS

According to history, the early Spanish explorers that visited the coast off of Islamorada noticed a purple hue from the lavender shells of sea snails and dubbed this Islamorada, which translates into "purple isles" in Spanish. Today, Islamorada is best known as being the sportfishing capital of the world. Here there are literally hundreds of charter boats which can transport the angler to offshore waters in search of billfish, dolphin, wahoo, kingfish and a wide variety of reef fish, or to the backcountry where tarpon, bonefish and permit are the favorite quarry on the flats.

The Village of Islamorada actually takes in several communities and keys. There are numerous marinas throughout this section of the islands, as well as famous resorts that are Keys landmarks. Dining and shopping opportunities abound, and while

Hand feeding huge tarpon at Robbie's Marina on Lower Matecumbe Key.

the emphasis may be on fishing, the snorkeling and diving is also outstanding.

Indian Key and Lignumvitae Key, near Lower Matecumbe Key, have become part of the state park system, and both feature interesting histories. South of Lower Matecumbe Key, Long Key State Park has one of the finest beaches in the Keys.

In the heart of the Keys is Marathon, reportedly named for the "marathon" task undertaken by workers building Henry Flagler's Overseas Railway. Marathon is located on Key Vaca and likely received its name through the Spanish phrase Cayos de Vacas, or cow keys. This probably referred to the large numbers of manatees or sea cows that were found in the surrounding waters.

Marathon is a bustling community with a wide choice of restaurants, activities, stores and shops, bars, fast food outlets and marinas. Cruisers traveling either Hawk Channel on the oceanside, or the ICW on Florida Bay, will both pass the famed Seven Mile Bridge while heading towards the Lower Keys.

LOWER KEYS AND KEY WEST

The hustle and bustle of Marathon sharply contrasts with the less populous lower Keys where the atmosphere is laid back in true Conch style. Bahia Honda Key boasts one of Florida's finest state parks where there is a marina, delightful beaches and many activities for the visitor. Nearby Big Pine Key, named for its stands of pine forest, is home to the National Key Deer Refuge and the Great White Heron National Wildlife Refuge. This area is a naturalist's paradise with hiking, beachcombing, birdwatching and kayaking being favorite pastimes. There are additionally many uncrowded anchorages and the backcountry fishing is unmatched. Fortunately, many of the outlying keys remain pristine and largely untouched.

Offshore is one of the Keys most popular diving and snorkeling sites, Looe Key. The coral formations found on this part of the reef are incredible and fish life abounds.

For many either cruising the Keys by boat or traveling by car, Key West represents the end of the journey. As one of the most visited destinations in the country, Key West offers something for everyone. The

dining and entertainment options are staggering and are available nearly around the clock. While being a major tourist destination, this city also has its share of history and culture. There are numerous museums and a great number of galleries featuring works created by local artists. The sunset celebration at Mallory Square is a must. A visit to Key West can be as exhausting or relaxing as your taste dictates.

Beyond Key West are the Dry Tortugas and Fort Jefferson that can only be visited with your own boat, ferry service or by seaplane charter. This historic fort is a marvel in itself and the surrounding waters are perfect for diving, snorkeling and fishing.

The Florida Keys and their famed waters provide an unparalleled diversity that make them one of the world's finest cruising grounds and vacation destinations.

Pumpkin Key anchorage in Biscayne Bay.

FISHING THE KEYS

by Harlan Franklin

I am a dyed-in-the-wool fisherman and my introduction to the Florida Keys could not have been more impressive. At first light Key West was barely in sight on the horizon after an overnight sail from Marco Island. As exciting as that sight was, another sight was just as attention grabbing. Spanish mackerel were everywhere, in all directions, as far as I could see. Thousands of them... leaping skyward, slashing through schools of silvery baitfish, turning the Gulf of Mexico's calm surface into a foamy sea of activity.

It was a simple matter to toss a jig out and snare a fresh mackerel for supper.

Fishing and diving are what the Florida Keys are about. It doesn't matter where in the Keys you are, there is good fishing nearby. If you tie up at a marina, chances are you can watch snapper, jack, barracuda and no telling what else swimming around your boat... if you're on the hook in an anchorage, the fish may not be so visible, but they are there.

The wide variety of fish available, both the tasty types and the sporty types, is hard to imagine. The cruising yachtsman dragging a spoon or jig behind the boat is very likely to hook a mackerel or kingfish. Another option available by dinghy is any of the hundreds of creeks and channels cutting through the mangrove islands and shallows. Here you'll find a wide variety of fish. Snapper, small grouper, bar jack, and mackerel all frequent these areas. A selection of D.O.A. lures, small jigs, or live shrimp all work great for these fish. Those boats equipped with freezer space might want to seek out a professional guide for a trip to the reef, where the prospects of multiple fish catches are common. Chances are your catch will include a limit of prized and great tasting yellowtail snapper. Sport fishing

Tarpon are the Silver King.

opportunities in the Keys are wide and varied. Bonefish, properly described as the gray ghost of the flats, can be found the length of the Keys. So can the wily permit, but these prestigious gamesters are more plentiful around the flats west of Key West. Barracuda and sharks also roam the shallow flats and both provide some interesting moments when the more sought after species become scarce. All these species will take a properly presented lure or fly. Even though a guide is not necessary, it is recommended. In selecting a guide for any purpose in the Keys, make inquiries among other anglers and ask for suggestions as to which guide to hire.

The Keys have become synonymous with tarpon. During spring and summer, fly fishermen line the edges of the flats and banks waiting for the silver king to appear. And they will appear, on both the Atlantic and Gulf and in between, all up and down the Keys.

Tarpon will first appear in large numbers early in the year, usually in January, in Key West's Northwest Channel. It is the opinion of many seasoned fishermen that Northwest Channel is the best place anywhere to catch a tarpon, better even than famed Boca Grande Pass upstate.

The odd thing is, the Keys are not widely thought of as a billfishing destination. They should be. Both sailfish and blue marlin are caught in surprising numbers. They can be taken on the Atlantic side anywhere along the Keys, from Key Largo to the Marquesas. The sailfish are usually found just off the reef and the marlin farther out. The waters off Key Largo have a great fall run of sailfish, as does Islamorada, Marathon and Key West. Twenty miles off Key West, a drop off called "Wood's Wall" is becoming well known as a marlin hotspot. Both sails and marlin are caught year round, though both have their hot periods. A recently rejuvenated and exciting fishery is for broadbill swordfish. Night fishermen drifting live bait or squid in the deep water outside Wood's Wall are finding excellent numbers of swordfish. Best attempt this on nights that are calm, clear and with little moonlight.

Fish, eating fish, catching fish, or just looking at fish... it's all a big part of the Florida Keys. When you arrive in the Keys, think like a native. Think fish.

Grouper grow big in the Florida Keys.
Photo Visit Florida

Skypic.Com

We offer one of the largest and most spectacular collections of scenic aerial photography from Maine to Cape Cod to New York, California, National Parks, Florida, the Florida Keys, the Bahamas, the Caribbean and the U.S. Virgin Islands.

Visit our cyberspace gallery to view thousands of beautiful aerials including colleges, sports events, lighthouses, ships, planes and much more. Available in hand printed photographs and murals up to 30" x 40". Also inquire about photographic assignments.

BENEATH THE SEAS

South Florida and the Keys are home to the only living coral reef in the United States and this distinction has made this group of islands the world's most visited diving location.

Encompassing an area largely from Key Biscayne through the Dry Tortugas, this reef system is incredibly complex and equally beautiful. As such a unique and valuable natural and recreational asset, it has been designated as the country's only marine preserve, the Florida Keys National Marine Sanctuary.

Different areas of the Keys coral reef also have their own unique characteristics. Some are known for their great abundance of fish life and others for spectacular coral formations, or a wide diversity of marine life. Wreck diving is additionally extremely popular.

Best of all the reef is accessible to both divers and snorkelers alike. For even the most advanced diver, the Keys provide challenging diving, and for the novice

Grey Angelfish

snorkeler, they are equally captivating.

Key Largo has named itself the dive capital of the world and here you will find more dive shops for its area than anywhere else. The famed John Pennekamp Coral Reef State Park is located in Key Largo and additionally another underwater namesake, the *Statue of Christ in the Abyss*. This statue of Christ, with its outstretched and welcoming arms, may be one of the single most photographed attractions by diving enthusiasts.

While Key Largo is a hub of much of the diving activity it certainly is not limited to this island. Nearly every community in your travels through the Keys have dive shops that offer daily boating tours, instruction and equipment rentals. You can also count on a high degree of professionalism and capabilities among the dive masters and instructors.

Besides the diving industry that revolves around the Keys, the coral reefs are widely used by the recreational boater. Fortunately, there has been an increased awareness of protection of the reef through a number of organizations, such as Reef Relief based in Key West.

This organization offers some of the following tips for the boater and fishermen:
• Before heading out, check weather conditions. Strong winds and rough seas can result in poor visibility and reduce safe interaction with the reef.
• Dumping trash at sea is illegal; plastic bags and other debris can injure or kill marine animals.
• Use sewage pumpout facilities if available and biodegradable bilge cleaner and never discharge sewage or bilgewater at the reef.
• Use reef moorings buoys or anchor in sandy areas away from coral and seagrasses so that anchor, chain and line

do not contact or damage coral or seagrasses.
• Accidental boat groundings damage the reef. Consult tide and navigational charts and steer clear of shallow areas.
• If you run aground immediately turn the engine off, and tilt it up if possible. Do not try to motor off. Wait until high tide to remove the vessel. Call for assistance when necessary.
• When in a dive area, slow down to an idle speed. Make sure the bow is down and the motor is not digging deep into the water.
• Fishermen, do not troll over or near divers. Stay at least 100 feet from the designated red and white diver down flags and watch for bubbles.
• Observe fishing size, bag limits and season closures when harvesting seafood. Release all the fish you cannot

Continued on Page 17

A snorkler on a Keys reef. Photo Visit Florida

Alligator Light marks Alligator Reef offshore of Upper Matecumbe Key.

The manatee, or sea cow, is found in Florida waters including throughout the Keys. Fortunately, their numbers have been rebounding, however, this gentle mammal is the center of controversy and that resulted in expanding boating regulations throughout the state. Obey the idle only speeds posted where manatees are known to be present. The laws are strictly enforced and fines are stiff. Photo Visit Florida

Continued from Page 15

eat. Consult marinas and local authorities for current regulations.

• Practice good seamanship and safe boating. Maintain safe distances from fishermen. Avoid wildlife disturbance; stay 100 yards or more offshore and keep speed, noise and wakes to a minimum near mangroves.

The following are some tips for divers and snorkelers.

• Snorkel aware and dive with care. Before booking a reef trip, check out weather conditions. It's best not to go out in rough seas. Poor visibility, strong winds and waves reduce safe interaction at the reef.

• Remember that even the slightest touch with hands or equipment can damage sensitive coral polyps. Avoid all contact from fins, hands and equipment.

• Snorkelers should wear float coats - inflatable snorkel vests - to allow gear adjustment without standing on the coral. Never stand up on a coral reef!

• To avoid contact with the ocean bottom, divers should only use the weight needed and practice proper buoyancy control.

• Avoid wearing gloves and touching or collecting marine life. Resist the temptation to feed the fish. It changes the natural behavior and the diet of the fish.

• Remember that it is illegal to harvest coral in Florida and many other places. Please don't harvest coral or buy coral souvenirs.

For further information on protecting coral reefs in the Keys and elsewhere throughout the world contact Reef Relief at 305-294-3100 or visit www.reefrelief.org.

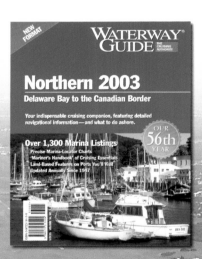

Western Union is a famous schooner berthed in Key West Bight's Historic Seaport. Photo Tom Henschel

GOVERNMENT CUT, MIAMI

GOVERNMENT CUT & MIAMI BEACH MARINA

South Beach

ATLANTIC OCEAN

NOT TO BE USED FOR NAVIGATION
Use as a reference only. Consult
recommended charts for navigation.

Fisher Island

Miami Beach Marina Office

Monty's Raw Bar, Neams Market, Hopkins Carter, Club Nautico & Tarpoon Lagoon Dive Center

U.S. Coast Guard

MacArthur Causeway

ASHORE

Almost immediately upon entering the cut, the Miami Beach Marina is found to starboard. This ultramodern facility in is the heart of chic South Beach and the famed Art Deco District. With approximately 400 slips, the marina can accommodate the largest of megayachts and is billed as being "the gateway to the Caribbean." Every possible amenity is found at this huge complex that provides concierge services and a tram on the grounds for transportation. Monty's Raw Bar with both inside and poolside seating for lunch and dinner is on site. In this main building you will additionally discover Neam's Market which is a gourmet grocery that also specializes in yacht provisioning, a Hopkins Carter Marine Hardware store with bait and tackle, the Tarpoon Lagoon Dive Center and a yacht brokerage. Other services available include a Club Nautico boat rentals, yacht and sportfishing charters, a casino cruise boat, Merrill Stevens emergency dockside service and 24-hour dock attendants.

This is all within a short walk or taxi ride to South Beach where entertainment, dining and shopping prospects abound nearly around the clock.

Miami Beach Marina provides immediate access to the Atlantic Ocean and the nearby Hawk Channel leading to the Florida Keys. Photo Tom Henschel

While not part of the Florida Keys, Government Cut has been included in this book as it is an important passage for many cruisers headed to the islands south of Miami. Government Cut is one of Florida's most easily navigated channels and Hawk Channel, which is the principal Atlantic Ocean route to Keys destinations, is readily accessed from this cut.

Likewise, this is a favorite stepping off point for the Bahamas and the islands of the Caribbean.

Government Cut is heavily utilized by both commercial and recreational vessels and also the numerous cruise ships that visit the Port of Miami. It can be extremely busy with heavy boating traffic.

NAVIGATION

As mentioned, Government Cut poses little challenge in the way of navigation, however, paying attention to other vessels utilizing the cut is essential. This is a deep and wide channel that is well-marked and is simply accessed from the ocean. Upon entering, much of the entire channel to the port on Dodge Island, is comprised of concrete bulkheads for cruise ships and commercial ships. An automobile ferry also transverses the cut on a regular basis from Miami Beach to the luxury residences of Fisher Island.

KEY BISCAYNE, CAPE FLORIDA

KEY BISCAYNE, CAPE FLORIDA

Miami Beach

KEY BISCAYNE

No Name Harbor

Village of Key Biscayne

Bill Baggs Cape Florida State Park

Cape Florida Lighthouse

Cape Florida Channel

CAPE FLORIDA

N

Shoals

NOT TO BE USED FOR NAVIGATION
Use as a reference only. Consult recommended charts for navigation.

wind directions. Another potential anchorage is found to the north of the harbor on the western shore of Key Biscayne. It provides fair shelter and again is a good stepping off point for cruises involving Atlantic routes.

ASHORE

The park lighthouse is open for tours and the adjoining beach is outstanding for sunbathing and swimming. Throughout the park you will find biking, hiking and skating paths along with attractive nature trails where native plant life has been restored. Fishing is a pastime of choice for anglers trying their luck from the seawalls along the Biscayne Bay side of the park. A concessionaire offers rentals of bicycles, kayaks, beach chairs and umbrellas.

Boaters making use of the harbor can visit the Boater's Grill in a two-story building with accompanying dockage for dinghies, however, do not expect much in the way of supplies for provisioning. Another open air restaurant, the Lighthouse Cafe, is found near the beach.

No Name Harbor offers outstanding shelter and is part of the Bill Baggs Cape Florida State Park. Modest park fees are charged for day and overnight anchoring.

The historic Cape Florida lighthouse, towering over the beaches of eastern Key Biscayne, holds the distinction of being the oldest standing structure in Miami-Dade County. The first lighthouse on the site was destroyed by Seminole Indians during the Second Seminole Indian War and the second tower which stands today was completed in 1846. The lighthouse is the signature attraction of the Bill Baggs Cape Florida State Park that is one of the most popular parks in the state. This park is also the home to an incredible beach that was once named as one of the top ten in the country. No Name Harbor within the park's grounds is widely utilized by boaters for day trips and overnighting with a modest fee for both.

NAVIGATION

The marked channel which flanks the western shore of Key Biscayne is an important passage for reaching Hawk Channel in the Atlantic, the main ocean route for traveling to the Keys. The channel follows the shoreline closely with noticeable shoals found to the southwest. There are also shoals off the tip of Cape Florida near the lighthouse. No Name Harbor is just off this channel and the anchorage is the perfect spot for spending the night before setting out for the Keys or the Bahamas. This harbor offers a safe refuge for waiting out poor weather, and offers protection from all

DINNER KEY & COCONUT GROVE

DINNER KEY &
COCONUT GROVE

Moorings

Coconut Grove
Sailing Club

Dinner
Key

Dinner Key
Marina

COCONUT GROVE

Scotty's
Restaurant

Grove Key Marina

Grove
Key
Marina

Monty's Raw
Bar & Marina

Coral Reef
Yacht Club

Dinner Key Channel

NOT TO BE USED FOR NAVIGATION
Use as a reference only. Consult
recommended charts for navigation.

ASHORE

Depending upon slip availability, you have several options for choices in marinas at Dinner Key. They include Monty's Marina, Grove Key Marina and Dinner Key Marina. If you are a member of a reciprocal yacht club, dockage may also be available at the Coral Reef Yacht Club, or Biscayne Bay Yacht Club. Monty's Marina has an excellent on site restaurant that has been a great success for many years, and Scotty's Landing Restaurant is adjacent to the Grove Key Marina.

For the cruiser, there are nearby grocery stores, liquor markets and marine stores for restocking. Any mechanical services are likewise readily available.

The downtown section of Coconut Grove is one of the reasons this part of Miami is so popular. Trendy shops offer everything ranging from antiques to formal wear, and a wealth of restaurants with an exciting nightlife are all part of the Coconut Grove scene. Don't plan to take it all in at one time. Around every corner you're sure to make a discovery that you would not have noticed on a quick tour.

Another view of the Dinner Key waterfront and Coconut Grove looking to the southwest.

D inner Key and Coconut Grove are the hub of South Florida's sailing activities, and especially sailboat racing. This is additionally an extremely desirable destination for the cruising boater with a large anchorage, fine marinas, incredible shopping and many restaurants. A great number of cruisers who have visited this section of Miami have decided to permanently call this home.

The anchorages are crowded with the widest variety of sailing vessels imaginable, many which may have been on the hook for years. These boats contrast sharply with the sleek and well maintained racing craft which you will find at area marinas and yacht clubs.

Coconut Grove

Cable
Area

G "5"
PA

Fl G
Priv

DINNER KEY CH

(use inset 2)

NAVIGATION

Dinner Key Channel, leading into the Dinner Key Marina which is a City of Miami property, can only be described as straight as an arrow. As long as you don't stray out of the channel onto the shoals, navigation could not be easier. The city hall is visible at the end of the channel. This is the primary route for access to the city marina and adjoining facilities. Another channel to the north leads to other marinas and yacht clubs. When in doubt, check your charts since there is considerable shoaling throughout this area and the adjoining anchorages.

ELLIOTT KEY

ELLIOTT KEY —
BISCAYNE NATIONAL PARK

BISCAYNE BAY

Beach

ELLIOTT
KEY

Marked Channel For
Marina Entrance

Marina

Park Ranger Station

Park Service
Docks

Restrooms
& Showers

NOT TO BE USED FOR NAVIGATION
Use as a reference only. Consult
recommended charts for navigation.

ASHORE

The park service operates marinas on Boca Chita Key (see aerial photo on Page 7) and Elliott Key where you can overnight for modest fees that are paid to ATM-like machines. You will have to do without water or electric hookups, although at Elliott Key there are showers and drinking water is available. The marina here is limited to boats with drafts of three feet or less and larger vessels must anchor offshore and dinghy into the harbor.

Elliott Key has been maintained largely in a natural state, while other islands to the north were once privately owned. Boca Chita has a distinctive lighthouse structure at the entrance to the harbor. Besides picnicking, swimming off the beach, and snorkeling, visitors can also camp on these islands in designated areas. Fish life abounds in the cuts separating the islands and there are excellent fishing spots. Likewise, the surrounding flats are a favorite among anglers in search of bonefish and other gamefish.

Sands Cut is a shallow water, small boat only passage between northern Elliott Key and Sands Key. It is a popular spot for swimming and snorkeling.

In the southern waters of Biscayne Bay lies one of the largest keys in the park system that encompasses this large and vastly popular bay for boating. Elliott Key and surrounding islands, including Boca Chita Key, Soldier Key, the Ragged Keys and Old Rhodes Key are all part of the Biscayne National Park which is managed by the National Park Service.

Just a short day sail from Miami marinas, or a quick powerboat ride away, the waters of these keys are usually crowded with weekend boaters. During the week you will likely have your pick of secluded anchorages or slips in the two park marinas located on the keys. There are numerous outstanding anchorages throughout the park and they are excellent spots for overnighting while en route to southern destinations.

NAVIGATION

The waters within this park have numerous banks and shoals, so deeper draft craft do need to exercise some caution. The Featherbed Bank is a large area of shoaling that runs east and west across a good portion of this area. Marked channels lead boaters through both East and West Featherbed Banks. Consult your charts for details and for water depths at planned anchorages. It is worthy to note that the western shores of these islands are exposed and anchorages can become uncomfortable during any heavy weather.

CARD SOUND

CARD SOUND BRIDGE
LITTLE CARD SOUND &
BARNES SOUND

Alabama
Jack's

Little Card
Point

Toll Plaza

LITTLE CARD
SOUND

Card Sound
Bridge

BARNES
SOUND

ICW

N

NOT TO BE USED FOR NAVIGATION
Use as a reference only. Consult
recommended charts for navigation.

guides as to recommended anchorages. Heading south, a channel just to the starboard under the Card Sound Bridge leads to Alabama Jack's. This channel is very narrow, but carries a depth adequate for most craft passaging on the ICW.

ASHORE

If your're hoping for a convenience store, or any shopping options at Card Sound, you need to pass on by. However, if your crew is in the mood for good food and a relaxing spell ashore, definitely make this sidetrip. Alabama Jack's is a crowded spot on weekends and a favorite stop for bikers that may be traveling to or from the Keys. Live country western music attracts large crowds on weekend afternoons. There is guest dockage which can handle most craft up to 40 feet, however, overnight slips are not available. Try the conch fritters, as they may be the best west of the Bahamas.

On the opposite side of the bridge is Crocodile Lake, part of the National Park's refuge for the American crocodile, a rarely seen endangered species.

Informal waterfront dining at Alabama Jack's at Card Sound.
Photo Tom Henschel

A roadside sign states "Welcome to downtown Card Sound", and while there is not much of a downtown, this is an interesting destination to visit. For years it had largely been occupied by squatters who had taken up residence here aboard boats or by building ramshackle homes that are still in evidence.

Card Sound is the first signs of civilization after passing through Biscayne National Park. It's certainly the first place where you can buy a cold drink or a meal. It is a rogue style community with a boundary that is outside the norm found in the suburbs to the north. Card Sound Bridge is the most noticeable feature that will be seen while traveling the sounds from Biscayne Bay. Unless you were aware of Alabama Jack's Restaurant to the starboard as you are heading south, it's likely that you would pass under the bridge without another thought of stopping.

NAVIGATION

This is the inshore route that represents the ICW passage to the Keys. The intracoastal follows a path from Biscayne Bay through Card Sound, Little Card Sound and Barnes Sound towards Jewfish Creek. It travels an easily navigated and well-marked channel, and there are several possible anchorages that provide protection in most weather conditions. Consult your charts and

BLACKWATER SOUND, GROUPER CREEK

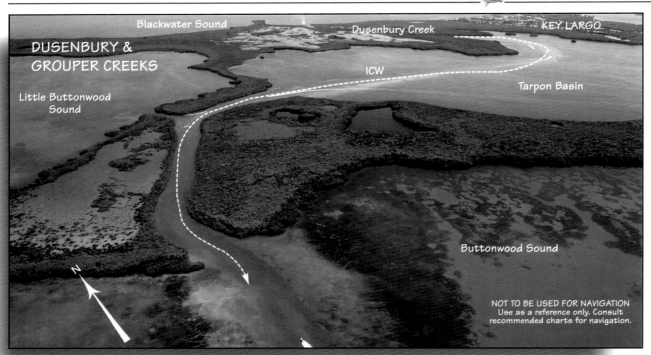

DUSENBURY & GROUPER CREEKS

Blackwater Sound

Dusenbury Creek

KEY LARGO

Little Buttonwood Sound

ICW

Tarpon Basin

Buttonwood Sound

NOT TO BE USED FOR NAVIGATION
Use as a reference only. Consult recommended charts for navigation.

the hustle and bustle of nearby U.S. 1. Consult your charts and guides for suggestions.

ASHORE

While Blackwater Sound, Tarpon Basin, Buttonwood Sound and this area's backcountry offer outstanding anchorages, there is an acute lack of marinas that cater to the cruising boat traffic. Most marinas found along the northern stretches of Key Largo's bayside are small and the emphasis is on serving the owners of trailerable boats. This contrasts with the Atlantic side of Key Largo where there are several marinas off Hawk Channel that welcome the larger transient boats.

If you are planning on an extended stay in this section of the Keys, it is possible to find an anchorage where you can dinghy in for provisions and also to sample the many fine restaurants that are found here.

The Marvin D. Adams Waterway represents a handy passage for smaller craft transiting between Blackwater Sound and Largo Sound. A fixed bridge of only 14 feet limits the size of vessels that can utilize this channel.

Traveling along the ICW through Blackwater Sound and into Dusenbury and Grouper Creeks is always a special experience if you are departing from points north. You know at this junction that you have really arrived in the Keys. The waters are usually sparkling clear in the creeks and nearly always you'll find fishermen aboard small boats anchored along the shoreline hoping for snapper or even a grouper. As the route winds through these mangrove shores, it's almost impossible to believe the highway is just a stone's throw away with its traffic, stoplights, strip malls, tourist shops and fast food restaurants. Instead you can

picture that this is the way you would like to see the Keys remain, and then realize it is wishful thinking.

NAVIGATION

There are no special challenges to navigating this area of the Intracoastal other than spotting markers and staying within the channel. If you have a draft in the five-foot range, you are likely to have some tense moments, but even boats drawing this much water should have little trouble. Keep a chart handy for reference and don't drift outside the channel. Slow down in the creeks and savor the moment, likewise, idle back for the many fishermen that you're bound to pass in these waters.

Anchoring possibilities abound throughout this area and it is possible to find secluded anchorages away from

KEY LARGO & LARGO SOUND

KEY LARGO & LARGO SOUND

Moorings

LARGO SOUND

John Pennekamp Coral Reef State Park Headquarters & Marina

El Radabob Key

South Sound Creek

Atlantic Ocean

Shoals

NOT TO BE USED FOR NAVIGATION. Use as a reference only. Consult recommended charts for navigation.

this narrow channel and especially the park's large sightseeing vessel.

ASHORE

Besides the moorings offered in Largo Sound, the park does have a limited number of slips located in the marina, where the headquarters are also found. Camping is another favorite pastime on the grounds and there is a relaxing beach for sunbathing or swimming. Dive and snorkel tours of the reef and glassbottom boats leave frequently throughout the day from the park marina.

For those desiring a wide selection in restaurants, more landside activities and nightlife, there are a few marinas located just off Hawk Channel between the park and Rodriguez Key. They include Key Largo Harbour with a repair facility, Marina del Mar Resort and Marina, Pilot House Marina and Mandalay Marina. Call ahead to make sure dockage is available.

Rodriguez Key lies just off Rock Harbor in Key Largo and offers fair weather anchorages. In the background is Dove Key.

Key Largo, known as the diving capital of the world, is also home to the John Pennekamp Coral Reef State Park. This is the country's only underwater park and it has attracted millions of visitors since it was established in the 1960's. On first impression, the park grounds themselves appear quite small, but it is the real estate below the surface that encompasses more than 50,000 acres that is the park's real attraction and treasure. Divers and snorkelers will discover several hundred different species of fish and more than fifty types of coral making up the ecosystem of the park's coral reef.

There are additionally a number of wrecks in the Key Largo area that are another attraction to divers.

NAVIGATION

Exercise care when operating your boat over these offshore reefs since there are shallow areas where you can easily run aground. This may cause damage to your vessel, but it is also bound to damage this fragile reef. You are responsible and fines can be extremely stiff for any damage to the reef, however accidental. Largo Sound does not allow anchoring and visiting boaters must take mooring provided by the park service. The moorings are available at a nominal fee and Largo Sound is a delightful spot for overnighting. When entering the South Sound Creek, keep aware of other boat traffic in

TAVERNIER COMMUNITY HARBOR

COMMUNITY HARBOR
& MANGROVE MARINA

Marked Channel
From ICW

Haulout
Facility

Marina Office
& Ships Store

Fuel
Dock

Bath House &
Laundry

Boat Ramp

Boat Storage

To US

NOT TO BE USED FOR NAVIGATION
Use as a reference only. Consult
recommended charts for navigation.

the option of anchoring, or heading into the marina. As mentioned, the depths in this anchorage are on the shallow side, however, if you are able to navigate the ICW without problems, you should not have trouble here.

ASHORE

Tavernier is an interesting, small community with a hardware store, shops, small restaurants and restored homes and buildings, such as the Tavernier Hotel pictured below.

A short walk from the marina is a major shopping center with a supermarket, banking, fast food outlets, a cinema, video rentals, Dillon's Pub & Grill, a liquor store and post office. One of the Keys major hospitals, Mariners, is adjacent to the shopping center.

The backcountry waters of this area are also worthy of exploration as there are many interesting small islands and numerous anchoring possibilities for those wishing to be on the hook.

The historic Tavernier Hotel was built in the 1930's and was originally a movie theater. Photo Tom Henschel

In the heart of Tavernier on Key Largo is a popular anchorage known as Community Harbor that is simply reached from the Intracoastal Waterway running through Florida Bay. This is a well-protected natural harbor that for the large part is surrounded by mangroves and a marina complex to the southeast. Mangrove Marina is one of the few facilities along this section of the ICW that is equipped to truly handle transient or cruising boats. Most marinas along this route tend to be operations on the small side and largely cater to smaller boats. Mangrove Marina has more than 100 slips, electric, water and

cable TV, a travel lift for haulouts, a ship's store and on site repairs. While the atmosphere could not be termed resort-style, it's a clean and quiet facility where renovation is continuing, and it is close to shopping and restaurants in Tavernier.

NAVIGATION

If your boat draws over four feet, waters entering the Community Harbor may be a tight squeeze, especially at low tide. The entrance to this harbor is marked and is found a short distance on a southerly course from Marker 64. The entrance is narrow and shoals with a new growth of mangroves that flank the channel. Pay close attention to the markers and stay mid channel to enter the harbor. Once inside, you'll have

TAVERNIER CREEK

Labels on photo:
Plantation Boat Mart
To ICW
Tavernier Creek Marina Office & Ship's Store
Conch Republic Divers
NOT TO BE USED FOR NAVIGATION
Use as a reference only. Consult recommended charts for navigation.
Cuda's Bait & Tackle
Las Brisas Cafe
Fixed Bridge Vert Cl 15 Ft
US 1
Dive Shops & Motels
TAVERNIER CREEK

the ICW. The markers at this intersection can be somewhat confusing, so utilize caution and study your charts if unfamiliar with the waters.

ASHORE

Partly because of the fixed bridge and additionally because there is not any transient dockage available along Tavernier Creek, this area holds little interest to cruising boaters traveling the Keys. However, it remains a hub of boating activity for smaller craft. The huge buildings of Tavernier Creek Marina house many boats in dry storage and on weekends and holidays it can be extremely busy here. Tavernier Creek Marina features a ship's store and gift shop, gas and diesel, the Las Brisas restaurant on the docks and Cuda's Bait & Tackle. Conch Republic Divers offer diving and snorkeling trips to the reef. At the nearby Plantation Boat Mart, the focus is also on smaller craft.

One of the best fishermen in the Keys.
Photo Tom Henschel

Tavernier Creek is a much used cut between Key Largo and Plantation Key connecting Florida Bay with the Atlantic. The western shore of this channel is heavily populated and packed with homes, while the opposite side remains largely mangroves. The creek is of no use to sailboats, or larger craft because of the fixed bridge spanning the channel. Regardless, traffic is usually heavy with small boats plying the channel on weekends.

Fishing and diving is excellent offshore along the reef here, and there are numerous dive shops and motels catering to the underwater fraternity. Molasses

Reef, Conch and Little Conch, Hen and Chickens, Crocker Reef and Davis Reef are just offshore along Hawk Channel and are all popular for fishing, diving and snorkeling.

NAVIGATION

Reaching Tavernier Creek from Hawk Channel is simply accomplished and is straightforward. The channel is well-marked into the creek, but as can be seen from the photo, you must stay within the channel because of the shoaling. The fixed U.S. 1 bridge has a vertical clearance of only 15 feet and the current can be swift through the creek. On the opposite side, the channel winds through housing developments and mangroves until it eventually exits and intersects with

LITTLE BASIN, WORLD WIDE SPORTSMAN

LITTLE BASIN & WORLD WIDE
SPORTSMAN'S BAYSIDE MARINA

LITTLE
BASIN

NOT TO BE USED FOR NAVIGATION
Use as a reference only. Consult
recommended charts for navigation.

Islamorada
Fish Company

World Wide Sportsman &
Zane Grey's Lounge

To Little Basin
Entrance & ICW

Marina

US 1

N

Little Basin on Upper Matecumbe Key is a popular anchorage among cruising boaters since it is well-protected, easily reached from the ICW and is close to a wide range of restaurants, shops and galleries, attractions and grocery stores. As part of the Village of Islamorada, which takes in several keys and towns, Upper Matecumbe also features a number of marina facilities that cater to transient boaters. Islamorada, which translates into the purple isles in Spanish, bills itself as the fishing capital of the world.

Throughout the waters surrounding this sprawling community you will always find fishermen on the flats, or aboard boats headed towards offshore fishing grounds. Additionally, here you will find several of the Keys most famous resorts, such as Cheeca Lodge and The Islander.

NAVIGATION

The entrance to Little Basin and its waters are on the shallow side. World Wide Sportsman Marina personnel recommend taking up a course of 163 degrees at Marker 84 on the ICW. At the entrance you will find Markers 1 and 2 leading into Little Basin. Inside depths range from three and a half to five feet at low tide and there is about a foot and a half tidal difference. This is a popular spot for anchoring for shallower draft boat owners. If you don't wish to dinghy ashore, head into the docks at World Wide

Sportsman's Bayside Marina, a recently constructed facility.

ASHORE

The World Wide Sportsman two-story complex is virtually a Disney World for the angler and boater. Here you will find aisles and display cases featuring the finest in sportfishing rods and reels, lures, books, clothing and sporting art. The centerpiece of the main floor is occupied by the sister ship to Ernest Hemingway's sportfishing vessel the *Pilar*. It has been beautifully restored and you can step aboard and visualize how sportfishing has changed in recent years. Upstairs is the Zane Grey Restaurant and Lounge with many original photographs of the famed author, letters and fishing gear he once utilized. Everything is displayed in a club-like setting with a porch overlooking the marina.

Next door is the Islamorada Fish Company which offers inside or marina front dining. Along U.S. 1 are numerous excellent restaurants including Sid & Roxie's famed Green Turtle Inn and Chef Lupe's Lazy Days. Other dining spots serve dishes ranging from sushi to Spanish or Italian cuisine. The nearby Lorelei Restaurant and Cabana Bar is a favorite gathering place for watching sunsets and for backcountry captains and anglers.

The sistership to Hemingway's sportfishing boat is a showpiece inside the World Wide Sportsman.
Photo Tom Henschel

UPPER MATECUMBE KEY, BUD N' MARY'S

Labels on image:
ICW
Cotton Key
Little Basin
Whale Harbor Channel
NOT TO BE USED FOR NAVIGATION
Use as a reference only. Consult
recommended charts for navigation.
N
Hampton Inn &
Outback Steak House
UPPER MATECUMBE KEY
Bud N' Mary's Dive Center
Lazy Days Bar & Seafood Grille
Ship's Store & Tackle Shop
Papa Joe's Restaurant & Marina
Bud N' Mary's High & Dry
Charter Boat Fleet

ASHORE

Although almost with certainty all the emphasis here is on fishing, there are a number of restaurants of interest. The best known is another Keys landmark, Papa Joe's across the street from Bud N' Mary's. Diners have been frequenting this establishment for many years and it is one of the few old time Keys-style restaurants remaining. Hundreds of fishing pictures decorate the walls of the dining room and lounge adding to the nostalgic atmosphere. Papa Joe's has a small marina, an upper deck lounge and boat rentals. Two other restaurants within walking distance are the Outback Steak House in the Hampton Inn and Lazy Day Bar and Seafood Grille. Besides accommodations at Bud N' Mary's, the Hampton Inn provides rooms and there are several other oceanfront resorts.

The Bud N' Mary's complex has an on site dive center offering reef diving and snorkeling trips, boat rentals and a fine bait and tackle shop also carrying ship's supplies.

A zoomed in view of the Bud N' Mary's Marina complex with its dry storage building, dockage, dive shop and bait and tackle store. Papa Joe's Restaurant and Marina is pictured across U.S. 1.

Bud N' Mary's Marina is one of the most famous destinations when it comes to sportfishing. The marina has been well-known for years as one of the best spots to charter a boat for offshore fishing in search of sailfish, dolphin, kingfish and reef fish. It is home to a sizeable charterboat fleet operated by some of the Key's most capable and productive captains. Waters offshore of Upper Matecumbe are noted for their outstanding angling prospects. Likewise, the backcountry is equally favorable for bonefish, tarpon, snook, redfish and other gamefish species. This marina also has numerous flats fishing guides available for this style of fishing.

NAVIGATION

Again, another fixed bridge here with only 10 feet of vertical clearance limits passage from the bayside to skiffs. Access to this marina must be made from the ocean into a marked channel leading into the two separate harbor areas. Indian Key Channel with a high bridge is located nearby to the west for boats traveling from Florida Bay. There are anchoring or mooring possibilities at Indian Key, Lignumvitae Key and Shell Key. All three islands are part of the state parks system.

INDIAN KEY CHANNEL

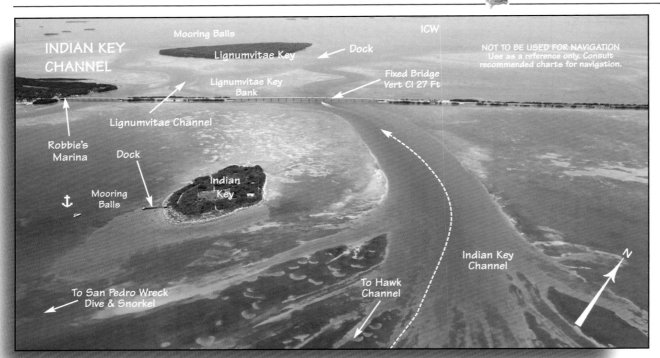

INDIAN KEY CHANNEL

Mooring Balls

Lignumvitae Key

ICW

Dock

NOT TO BE USED FOR NAVIGATION
Use as a reference only. Consult
recommended charts for navigation.

Lignumvitae Key Bank

Fixed Bridge
Vert Cl 27 Ft

Lignumvitae Channel

Robbie's Marina

Dock

Mooring Balls

Indian Key

Indian Key Channel

To San Pedro Wreck
Dive & Snorkel

To Hawk Channel

N

dependent upon your draft. Lignumvitae Channel to the west is only suited for smaller boats since it has a fixed bridge with only 10 feet of clearance.

ASHORE

A visit to Robbie's Marina on Lignumvitae Channel is entertaining just to take in the spectacle of huge tarpon, numbering in the hundreds, virtually being hand fed. Over the years the tarpon have been attracted to the docks by this handout and their aggressive feeding is a sight to see. (See Page 10) For a small fee you can buy a bucket of bait and take part.

Robbie's is a small marina and takes transient boats, but slips are usually limited. Make reservations ahead of time if you hope to visit with your own boat. This marina is popular among boat trailering fishermen and there are accommodations nearby. Kayaks and other boats can be rented and there is a restaurant appropriately named the Hungry Tarpon that serves three meals a day adjacent to the marina.

A closeup aerial view of Indian Key and its ruins. The key is also found on the cover of this book.

O f all the islands in the Keys, Indian Key has among the most historic, bloody and fascinating pasts. It has been home to native American Indians, a thriving community was once built here largely based on the wrecking trade, it was once designated as the Dade County seat of government, it was the site of a massacre, once a home to a famed botanist and ultimately it has become part of Florida's state park system. Its history is so colorful that it could be scripted as a movie.

More can be learned about the island's past by taking a tour, and while there is not a great deal to see, learning more about Indian Key is worthwhile. Stop by Robbie's Marina at the tip of Lower Matecumbe Key for tour information to both Indian Key and Lignumvitae Key, another interesting state park island.

NAVIGATION

Indian Key Channel is well-marked as it snakes through shoals and banks on both sides of the bridge. If you pay attention to the channel aids and utilize your eyesight for navigating, it poses no problems as a passage. A fixed bridge at 27 feet unfortunately limits use of the channel. Anchorages and moorings are found at both Lignumvitae and Indian Keys. Visitors to either island can also use guest dockage that is largely

LOWER MATECUMBE KEY

LOWER MATECUMBE KEY

Channel Five

Channel Two

True Value Hardware

Caloosa Cove Marina

Bait & Tackle Shop

Convenience Store

Captain's Table Restaurant

Safari Lounge

Beach

Caloosa Cove Oceanfront Resort

U.S. 1

NOT TO BE USED FOR NAVIGATION
Use as a reference only. Consult recommended charts for navigation.

N

also a marina that accepts transient boats. Another anchorage can be found in Matecumbe harbor in Florida Bay.

ASHORE

If you have a desire to stay ashore for a night, Caloosa Cove Resort adjoining the marina offers luxury ocean-front accommodations in 30 condominiums, complete with a large pool, a small beach and tennis courts. The Safari Lounge overlooks the ocean with grand views from its patio and features a unique decor with many mounted trophies and photographs that were taken during African safaris. The lounge offers package goods. For breakfast, lunch and dinner visit the Captain's Table on the marina grounds.

As a part of this complex there is additionally a well-stocked bait and tackle shop, a convenience store and a True Value Hardware shop that has many marine supplies. Boats can be rented from the marina.

Across U.S. 1 is the Florida National High Adventure Sea Base connected with the Boy Scouts.

The huge mural on Caloosa Cove's dry-storage building overlooks the marina harbor. Photo Tom Henschel

There are few marinas in the Keys that offer the immediate access to the ocean that is found at Caloosa Cove Marina, and it's one of the reasons it is popular among charterboat captains and small craft fishermen. The building for dry storage at this marina is painted with an interesting mural featuring a scene depicting life among the Indians who once populated these islands. The painting is extremely well done and must have presented a sizeable challenge for the artist. It overlooks the small harbor which is home to several charter vessels.

NAVIGATION

The channel leading into the marina is well-marked, deep, and navigation is straight forward from Hawk Channel. Unfortunately a fixed bridge at Channel Two limits passage to Florida Bay to only back-country boats. However, just a short distance to the west is Channel Five, which represents one of the most important passages in the Lower Keys for transiting back and forth between the ocean and Florida Bay waters. Channel Five is an easily navigated passage with deep water and a bridge with a vertical clearance of 65 feet. This channel is adjacent to Long Key Bight on the ocean, which offers possibilities for anchoring. Fiesta Key is nearby, and although this is an RV park, there is

HAWK'S CAY RESORT & MARINA

DUCK KEY & HAWK'S CAY RESORT & MARINA

Toms Harbor Keys

Duck Key Marina

Hawk's Cay Main Marina

NOT TO BE USED FOR NAVIGATION
Use as a reference only. Consult recommended charts for navigation.

U.S. 1

WatersEdge Restaurant

Dolphin Connection At Hawk's Cay

The Inn At Hawk's Cay

Small Boat Basin

Enter Channel From Ocean

marina is from Hawks Channel since bridges from Florida Bay are very limited in vertical clearance, the exception being the bridge at Channel Five at the north end of Long Key. From the ocean a privately marked channel leads into the marina traveling between a breakwater to the starboard and homes to the port. The current can be swift in the channel. Hail the marina on VHF 16 should you have questions. Reservations are also advised at this popular port of call.

ASHORE

The marina features an outstanding ship's store and most of the resort's watersports concessions are located along the docks. The WatersEdge restaurant and lounge overlooks the marina and serves up seafood with a variety of other dishes.

Nearby is the Duck Key Plaza which has a bank, a realtor, the Duck Key Emporium deli and All That Glitters jewelry store. That's largely the extent of your shopping prospects on the island, other than resort shops.

Duck Key Marina is another boating facility on the island and it caters largely to smaller boats. It has a ship's store, service and parts department, a dry storage barn, fuel and offers boat rentals.

A dolphin enjoys the company of visitors and a trainer at the Hawk's Cay Dolphin Connection. Photo Hawk's Cay Resort

Duck Key is home to one of the Keys premiere vacation facilities, Hawk's Cay Resort and Marina, a huge complex that offers visitors a luxurious life-style that rivals any on the mainland. With its close proximity to the ocean waters for sportfishing and diving or snorkeling, the 85-slip Hawk's Cay Marina has long been a choice port of call for boaters traveling to the Keys. Much of this small island is occupied by high end homes and it lacks the commercialism that is so evident throughout much of the Keys. The grounds of the island are meticulously kept and the atmosphere is more akin to what you might find in Palm Beach rather than the laid-back Keys. The resort has provided visitors with every conceivable activity possible from the Indies Spa to the Dolphin Connection. There is a wealth of watersports programs available including Colgate's Offshore Sailing School, offshore and backcountry fishing charters, boat and watercraft rentals, daily cruises, parasailing and snorkeling and diving instruction or excursions from Tilden's Scuba Center. Combine this with six restaurants, a number of lounges and top shelf accommodations, and you will find visitors are likely to discover they have little desire to leave the island while vacationing.

NAVIGATION

For most boaters, the only route to approach the

KEY COLONY BEACH

VACA KEY

Vaca Cut

Boat House Marina

Island Tiki Bar & Restaurant

N

Captain Hook's Marina & Dive Center

Key Colony Beach Marina & Charter Fleet

Quarterdeck Restaurant

KEY COLONY

Bonefish Marina

Bonefish Towers

Coco Plum Beach

COCO PLUM BEACH & KEY COLONY BEACH

NOT TO BE USED FOR NAVIGATION
Use as a reference only. Consult
recommended charts for navigation.

prior arrangements. Farther into the harbor you will find the Key Colony Beach Marina. The marina offers transient slips and features a tackle shop boat rentals and fuel. A Deep Blue Dive Center is located on the premises and the Quarterdeck Restaurant serves lunch and dinner. Adjacent to the marina is a strip mall with limited groceries available and a deli. Small boat dockage can be found at the Holiday Inn Marina if you are a hotel guest, and adjoining the facility is the Abyss Dive Center.

Just to the west before reaching Marathon is Vaca Cut pictured below. The current is usually swift through this channel, so be prepared. The Boat House Marina to starboard caters mostly to smaller boats with a large high and dry facility. Just before the bridge to the port is Captain Hook's Marina (both shown below), however, there are no transient slips available. This is a dive operation and fishing center for charter and party boats.

Vaca Cut is used by smaller craft because of the fixed bridge. The current runs swiftly through this channel.

C oco Plum Beach and Key Colony Beach are heavily residential areas with a good number of motels and beachfront resorts scattered throughout the communities. There is little opportunity for anchoring in this section of the Keys and slips for transient cruising boats are likely to be in short supply.

Nonetheless, should you be able to find dockage, this is a pleasant stopover on a Keys cruise. It is a quiet community with a few restaurants and shops, and it is close to Marathon for airport transportation, grocery stores, provisioning and marine supply stores.

NAVIGATION

Accessed from Hawk Channel on the Atlantic, an easily spotted landmark for the cut entrance is the high-rise Bonefish Towers condominium building. This building can be spotted from a good distance away and is located on the eastern shore of the channel leading into Key Colony Beach. Another channel that is widely utilized for crossing from the ocean to the bayside waters is Vaca Cut, however, a fixed bridge limits the size of a vessel making the passage.

ASHORE

The first possibility for dockage when entering the channel is at the Bonefish Marina, and while these slips are privately owned, sometimes space is available with

BOOT KEY HARBOR, MARATHON

Atlantic Ocean
VACA KEY, MARATHON & BOOT KEY HARBOR
Boot Key
Faro Blanco Marine Resort Bayside
Moorings
Shoals
Sister Creek
BOOT KEY HARBOR
Sombrero Marina & Dockside Lounge
Marathon City Marina
Sombrero Reef Explorers
Cannon Marina
Home Depot
US 1
N
NOT TO BE USED FOR NAVIGATION Use as a reference only. Consult recommended charts for navigation.
Sombrero Resort & Lighthouse Marina

ASHORE

Boot Key Harbor features several excellent marinas with a wide variety of amenities and several are mentioned accompanying the smaller photo below. Farther into the harbor you will find the Boot Key Harbor City Marina, which also offers pumpouts and dinghy dockage, the Sombrero Marina and Dockside Lounge, and the Sombrero Resort and Lighthouse Marina. The Dockside Lounge provides excellent food, live entertainment every evening of the week, and is the favorite gathering spot for cruisers and liveaboards. You'll find a resort atmosphere with a pool, tennis courts, accommodations, a tiki bar, restaurant and gift shop at the Sombrero Resort and Lighthouse Marina. Sombrero Reef Explorers is the on site dive shop offering private snorkeling trips as well as sunset cruises.

Throughout Marathon are a wide spectrum of restaurants, enough to satisfy any dining desires. Marine supplies and repair services are readily available.

A view from oceanside overlooking the entrance to Boot Key Harbor. The first boating complex to the port entering the channel is Marathon Marina. Immediately after the L-shaped mangrove formation is Pancho's Fuel Dock, then Burdine's Waterfront Marina and Faro Blanco Bayside to the far right of the photo. Seven Mile Marina and Turnkey Marina are located on the western tip of Vaca Key on the bayside.

Boot Key Harbor in the heart of Marathon has long been one of the most heavily populated harbors in the Florida Keys. It is well protected and does accommodate a great number of cruising and liveaboard boats, especially during the winter months. However, along with the harbor's popularity has arisen some controversy. There are efforts being made to "clean up" the atmosphere and crack down on those who violate overboard waste laws. Anchoring may one day become a life-style of the past in the harbor with increasing emphasis being placed on paid moorings. There is never likely to be a happy or equitable solution, but meanwhile life goes on in this colorful community of cruisers and liveaboards.

NAVIGATION

The harbor can be entered through two channels, one at Sister Creek on the oceanside and the other to the west at the beginning of the Seven Mile Bridge. The channels are well-marked, but take some unexpected turns, and if you are visiting for the first time, consult your charts. Once inside the harbor, you will discover some shoal areas and efforts to rebuild seagrass beds. Should you plan on anchoring out, try to find a spot with adequate swing room and make sure your anchor is firmly planted in case of a blow. You are certain to have a great deal of company.

SUNSHINE & BAHIA HONDA KEYS

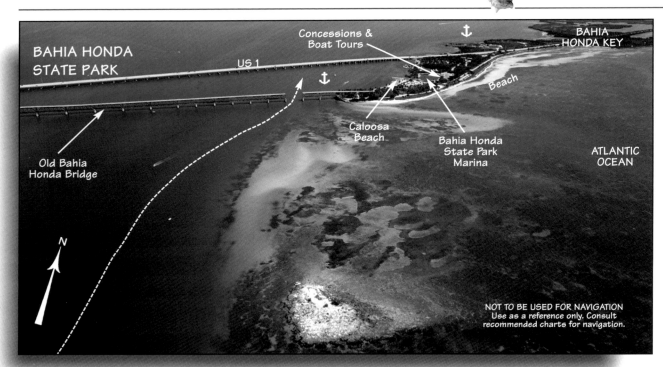

BAHIA HONDA
STATE PARK

US 1

Concessions &
Boat Tours

BAHIA
HONDA KEY

Beach

Old Bahia
Honda Bridge

Caloosa
Beach

Bahia Honda
State Park
Marina

ATLANTIC
OCEAN

N

NOT TO BE USED FOR NAVIGATION
Use as a reference only. Consult
recommended charts for navigation.

weather conditions, and it is worth noting that the current can be extremely swift. As shown in the photo, another anchorage on the bayside may be more protected, depending upon wind direction and strength.

ASHORE

The park is ideally suited for just relaxing along the beach shores under the shade of a palm tree or sunbathing in the sand. Because of the shallow waters surrounding much of the park, it is perfect for snorkeling and swimming from the shore. The flats found along the shoreline are great for the wading fly fisherman.

The park marina does provide dockage for transient boats in a well-protected harbor with 30 amp electricity, waste pump out and water. A concession building is a short walk and here you will find bait and tackle, a limited supply of groceries, gifts, a snack bar and ice. A tour boat offers daily snorkeling trips to Looe Key reef.

Another marina accepting transients is Sunshine Key, immediately to the northeast. This marina is part of the Sunshine Key Fun Resort, an RV park, and is consequently mostly served by smaller craft.

Sunshine Key Resort and Marina is located on Florida Bay and has dockage available for transient boats.

Bahia Honda State Park is one of the finest facilities of its kind that you will find in the Keys, or for that matter the mainland. It occupies around 500 acres and was once part of Henry Flagler's East Coast Railway project that began in 1905. A new bridge now serves travelers on U.S. 1, but at the park a portion of the Old Bahia Honda Bridge has been preserved and offers visitors a dramatic viewing post overlooking the Atlantic Ocean and Florida Bay.

With miles of some of the best beaches found in the Keys, the park offers outstanding swimming, snorkeling and beachcombing. Additionally

overnight lodging is available, camping, bicycling, fishing, picnicking, kayaking and there is a marina. It is a widely utilized park among visitors and residents of the Keys alike.

NAVIGATION

Bahia Honda Channel is one of the deepest natural passages in the Keys and it is a good choice for moving between the Atlantic waters and Florida Bay, unless you are a sailboat or other vessel that requires more than 20 feet of clearance. The newly constructed bridge is fixed at this vertical clearance, however, the good news is a portion of the old bridge has been cut away to allow boats into an anchorage between the spans with access to the park. This anchorage can be a bit rough in some

NEWFOUND HARBOR CHANNEL

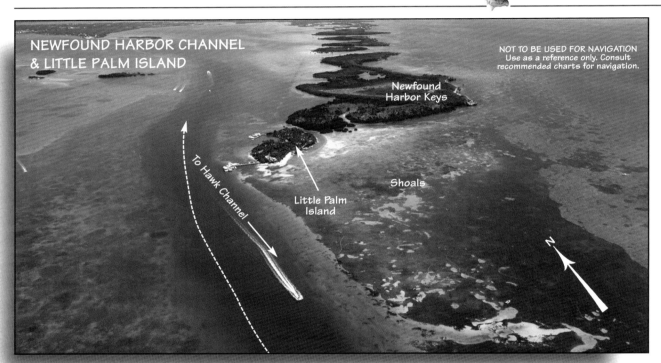

NEWFOUND HARBOR CHANNEL
& LITTLE PALM ISLAND

NOT TO BE USED FOR NAVIGATION
Use as a reference only. Consult
recommended charts for navigation.

Newfound
Harbor Keys

To Hawk Channel

Little Palm
Island

Shoals

N

ASHORE

Immediately upon entering the channel, Little Palm Island will be found to the starboard. This once was the site of a fishing camp that had hosted a number of U.S. presidents and other notables, as well as being used for the filming of the movie PT 109. It is now the exclusive Little Palm Island Resort & Spa and can only be reached by boat or seaplane. Accommodations are available in 28 thatched roof bungalows on the shores of the island, and the resort restaurant is known for its gourmet dining. Guests and visitors are ferried from a facility on Little Torch Key.

Cruising craft with a modest draft can be accommodated overnight at the Dolphin Resort and Marina on Little Torch Key just before the 15-foot fixed bridge for U.S. 1. The Keys Sea Center is another marina located across the channel on Big Pine Key, however, it caters to smaller boats and does not have slips for transients.

Once known as Munson Island, Little Palm Island is the site for the exclusive Little Palm Island Resort & Spa. Luxury accommodations are available in thatched roof, waterfront bungalows.

The upper reaches of Newfound Harbor Channel offer several fine anchoring prospects for boats traveling on the Atlantic side along Hawk Channel, however dockage in this region is somewhat limited. This is especially true for deeper draft vessels.

There are attractions that make a visit to this area worthwhile, including the nearby the Looe Key National Marine Sanctuary which is regarded as one of the premier diving and snorkeling sites in the Keys. Named for the H.M.S. Looe, a British ship wrecked in the 1700's, it is known for incredible staghorn coral formations that are found nearly at the

water's surface. Deeper canyons abound throughout the coral making this dive ideal for both beginners and advanced divers alike.

It will require auto transportation, but a visit to the Key Deer National Wildlife Refuge on Big Pine Key and No Name Key should be considered. Here you will discover the endangered Key deer that stand at only a couple of feet tall.

NAVIGATION

Newfound Harbor Channel is easily navigated and anchorages can be found in Newfound Harbor and along the shores of both Little Torch Key to the Port and Big Pine Key to starboard. The channel provides fair protection in most weather conditions.

STOCK ISLAND & OCEANSIDE MARINA

-STOCK ISLAND-

Peninsular Marine

Boat Ramp

Florida Keys Boat Center

Hickory House Restaurant

Marina Office & Ships Store

High & Dry Storage

Marina

NOT TO BE USED FOR NAVIGATION
Use as a reference only. Consult
recommended charts for navigation.

Channel offers well-protected anchoring and there are a good number of boats with their hooks permanently set.

ASHORE

Oceanside Marina caters to cruising boaters and the facility is second to none, however, sportfishing is likewise taken very seriously here. In fact, Oceanside is home to more world record gamefish catches than any marina in the country. It is also an important stepping off point for Cuba, Mexico or points south in the Caribbean. There is fuel on site, a ship's store with bait and tackle, huge dry storage barns, boat ramps and showers. Adjoining the Oceanside complex are boating related businesses and the Florida Keys Boat Center. The Peninsular boatyard is within walking distance and is a widely utilized yard among cruisers.

Two Stock Island restaurants that deserve note are the Rusty Anchor and Hickory House. The Rusty Anchor is part of a commercial seafood operation and you can depend on your seafood choices to be caught that day. The restaurant is a favorite among Key West locals. Hickory House is across the street from Oceanside Marina and features a Keys character served up with excellent food and a comfortable lounge.

Sunset Marina, not shown in these aerial photos, is a new marina located on the Gulf side of Stock Island. This marina provides transient and permanent dockage, a grocery store, fuel, a marine service shop and other amenities.

S tock Island lacks the glamor and glitz of its neighboring Key West and is more of a "working man's" island. On first impression this community is a hodgepodge of warehouses, trailer parks, commercial docks filled with lobster and stone crab boats, boat builders, convenience stores and other buildings. All of this contrasts sharply with the high-dollar condominiums which border the ocean.

Stock Island has humble beginnings and history records the island was utilized as a stockyard of sorts for barnyard animals that were ultimately

served up on menus in Key West. You can grow tired of seafood!

Appearances aside, Stock Island does feature one of the finest boating facilities in the Keys, Oceanside Marina, and an excellent boatyard, especially for do-it-yourselfers, Peninsular Marine Enterprises.

NAVIGATION

Oceanside Marina and the Peninsular boatyard are both easily reached from well-marked channels leading from the Atlantic. Nearby Boca Chica Channel heads to an intersection with U.S. 1 and there you will find Murray Marine, (not shown in photo) which largely caters to smaller boats and backcountry fishing guides or diving charters. The waters flanking Boca Chica

Permit are high on the hit list as a target for sportfishing anglers fishing Key West waters. Photo Harlan Franklin

KEY WEST

NOT TO BE USED FOR NAVIGATION
Use as a reference only. Consult
recommended charts for navigation.

KEY WEST
Moorings
U.S.C.G.
Conch Harbor
Marina
The Galleon
Resort & Marina
Hyatt
Key West
Pier House
Ocean Key
Resort
Mallory Square
Key West Airport
Garrison Bight City Marina
Key West's
Historic Seaport
A&B Marina
Key West Bight
Customs House
Arts & History
Museum
Key West
Aquarium
Hilton
Key West

west Channel represents the favored passage. There are several mooring and anchorage areas near downtown and the Key West Bight, however, during any season you can expect they will be crowded.

ASHORE

Entire books have been published on visiting Key West, and the bars, restaurants, attractions, museums, and hotels are much too numerous to mention here. However, regardless of your interests, dining pleasures or plans for a night on the town, you can count on finding it in Key West. Visit the Chamber of Commerce for maps and other information. Don't miss the tradition of the sunset party at Mallory Square on the waterfront, and if you want to take in much of the city in a short time, board one of the many trolleys or Conch Trains that journey throughout the neighboring streets.

If you are not planning on anchoring out, or taking a city mooring, you have a choice of several marinas including the the Conch Harbor Marina, the Galleon Marina, A & B Marina, Key West Bight Marina, and the Hilton Key West Resort and Marina, which are all located within walking distance of downtown. Other choices include marinas centered around the Garrison Bight area.

Sunsets are taken seriously in the close of the day's celebration at Mallory Square on the waterfront. Photo Tom Henschel.

Key West has a wide diversity of cultures, a rich and fascinating history, sparkling clear waters, attractive beaches, wide choices in dining, exciting nightlife and many attractions that make this city one of the country's most popular vacation destinations. Key West is literally at the end of the road, being the southernmost city in the U.S., and it is closer in proximity to Havana than Miami.

Because of its colorful flavor and climate, Key West has attracted many literary and creative types in years past included famed writers Ernest Hemingway, Tennessee Williams and Robert Frost. Among other notable individuals, President Harry Truman

vacationed in the "Little White House" located on Front Street. The extensive history of this city and its ties with the sea are evident while touring the Old Town section and other areas.

While popular among vacationers, Key West is an equally desirable destination for cruising boaters, sportfishermen and divers. Prior reservations for dockage at the local marinas are most often a must.

NAVIGATION

Key West Harbor is reached from the ocean by a well-marked, deep and wide Main Ship's Channel. This is negotiated by large cruise ships and poses little challenge after consulting your charts. For those traveling from Gulf of Mexico waters, North-

KEY WEST BIGHT & SEAPORT

KEY WEST BIGHT & HISTORIC SEAPORT

NOT TO BE USED FOR NAVIGATION. Use as a reference only. Consult recommended charts for navigation.

Ferry Terminal

City Marina

Schooner Wharf

Turtle Kraal

A&B Marina

Conch Harbor Marina

Breakwater

Waterfront Market

The Galleon Marina

Conch Republic Seafood

The Galleon

Bight's turning basin with its marinas and dockage.

ASHORE

The Seaport boasts several waterfront restaurants and bars including the Conch Republic Seafood Company, Half Shell Raw Bar, Turtle Kraals and Schooners Wharf Bar. Most provide live music and you can always count on lively crowds most afternoons and evenings.

Shoppers won't be disappointed since there are several interesting shops and galleries on the waterfront, and the Waterfront Market is well-known for its seafood, produce and deli. Numerous events, such as Key West Race Week and the Conch Republic Independence Celebration, are staged from this harbor.

Visiting boaters should always make reservations well in advance for berths as dockage is in high demand at the popular marinas which include the Galleon Marina, a resort-style complex, the A&B Marina, Conch Harbor Marina, and the City Marina at Key West Bight. The Seaport is the hub of a great deal of Key West's activities and these marinas put you in the heart of the action.

A view of the anchorage and mooring area near Sunset Key in the foreground, Wisteria Island and the Bight entrance far right.

K ey West Bight was once the center of a booming shrimping industry and much of the dockage and waterfront was occupied by hundreds of shrimp boats that were berthed in the harbor.

The city bought much of the property in the Bight in the early 90's and it has since been transformed into an attraction in itself, Key West's Historic Seaport and Harborwalk. The shrimping fleet has since relocated to Safe Harbor on Stock Island. The maritime flavor surrounding the Bight has been preserved since it has become the home port for a number of classic vessels and tall ships, all of which provide visitors

with a wide variety of cruises. The Seaport is the base for much of the city's fishing charter fleet, sailing, snorkeling and diving excursions and ferry boat services to the Dry Tortugas plus high-speed round-trip ferries between Fort Myers, Miami and Key West.

NAVIGATION

The Key West Bight Channel is deep and wide and presents no navigational challenges, however, you can expect heavy traffic throughout the Bight on almost any day, and especially weekends. Besides the recreational vessels, there are the many tourism oriented craft and commercial boats that utilize the waters of the Bight at all times of the day. A breakwater and lighted marker signal the entrance into the

BOCA GRANDE & MARQUESAS KEYS

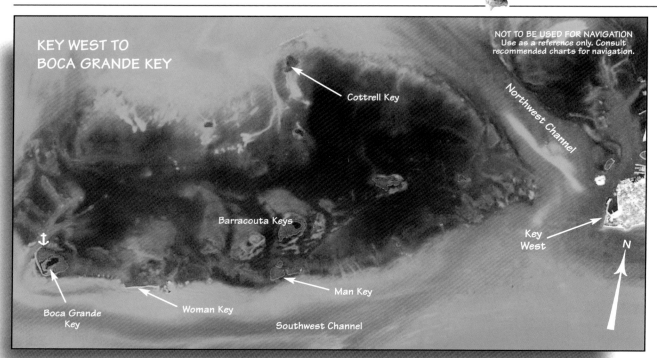

KEY WEST TO
BOCA GRANDE KEY

NOT TO BE USED FOR NAVIGATION
Use as a reference only. Consult
recommended charts for navigation.

Cottrell Key

Northwest Channel

Barracouta Keys

Key
West

N

Man Key

Boca Grande
Key

Woman Key

Southwest Channel

are essential for navigating these waters. Good light is also helpful for spotting channel markers, heads and shoals.

The anchorage for Boca Grande Key is located in the channel at the northwestern reaches of the island. Mooney Harbor in the Marquesas Keys offers other anchoring options. Use a good deal of care when entering either of these anchorages by keeping a sharp lookout and studying charts. As mentioned, neither of these destinations are safely navigated or suitable for anchoring in any heavy weather or poor visibility.

ASHORE

This group of keys are noted for its excellent flats fishing including permit, bonefish and tarpon. There is also excellent snorkeling and exploration aboard your dinghy. The anchorages can also be "buggy", so be prepared.

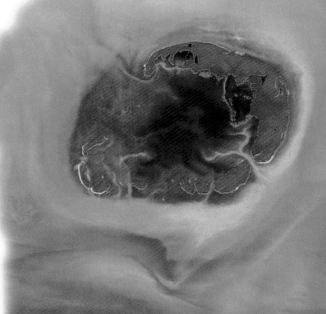

The Marquesas Keys as viewed from satellite.

For cruisers with an adventurous streak and those who are seeking the solitude and beauty of almost untouched islands, a visit to the Boca Grande and Marquesas Keys is especially worthwhile. This group of keys are also a logical stopover for anyone cruising to the Dry Tortugas and Fort Jefferson since this destination is about 70 miles from Key West. But this is not all without sacrifice because you will be leaving the comfort of docks and electricity, grocery stores and restaurants, fuel and ice all behind in Key West. These keys are much like they would have been found hundreds of years ago and they are largely unspoiled.

A visit here requires a good deal of prior planning, and careful consideration as weather conditions must be heeded because there are few places safely providing shelter during frequent blows which sweep these islands.

NAVIGATION

As is evident from the two accompanying satellite images, these keys are surrounded by shoals, reef formations, coral heads and meandering channels that often dead end. Anchorages at Boca Grande Key and the Marquesas Keys can either be reached from Hawk Channel heading west along the chain of islands on the ocean side, or via the northern route along the Northwest Channel. Weather at the time will dictate which route is the best for your voyage. Detailed charts and the advice offered by other Keys guides

MARQUESAS
KEYS

Mooney
Harbor

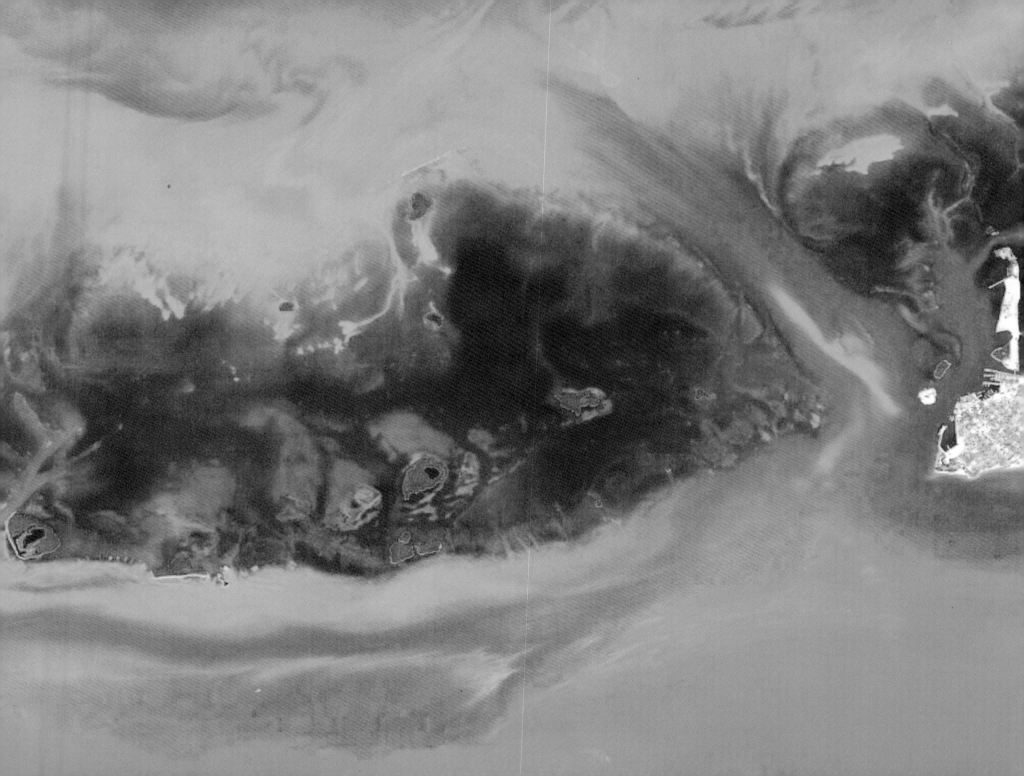

DRY TORTUGAS, FORT JEFFERSON

GARDEN KEY &
FORT JEFFERSON

FORT
JEFFERSON

Park & Ferry
Docks

NOT TO BE USED FOR NAVIGATION
Use as a reference only. Consult
recommended charts for navigation.

Tortugas in daylight hours before anchoring up for the night. Channels leading into the Garden Key anchorage are well marked.

ASHORE

A self-guided tour of Fort Jefferson is a must for any visitor and park personnel are especially helpful. After taking in the fort, you have your choice of sunbathing on the spectacular beaches, or diving into the crystal clear waters and enjoying some of the finest snorkeling that can be found anywhere. Birdwatching is another favorite pastime as up to 200 different varieties can be spotted on the islands during various times of the year. As you would expect for a more remote area, the fishing is outstanding.

Fort Jefferson and Garden Key opposite page. Photo Visit Florida
A seaplane flys over Bush Key (below) on an approach to a landing at Garden Key. Photo Seaplanes of Key West

Steeped in a colorful history, a visit to Dry Tortugas and Fort Jefferson represents a fascinating step back into time. This group of islands, laying approximately 70 miles west of Key West was discovered by the Spanish explorer Ponce de Leon in 1513 and were named "Las Tortugas" (the turtles) because of their population of sea turtles. "Dry" was later added to their name warning sailors of a lack of water.

In 1825 a lighthouse was first built on Garden Key and construction of Fort Jefferson began in 1846 and continued for 30 years. The fort was never completely finished, however, it is remark-

ably well preserved and has been declared a national monument. The Dry Tortugas were designated as a national park about a decade ago.

The only means of reaching this park is either aboard your own boat, high speed ferries, or seaplanes departing on a regular basis from Key West.

NAVIGATION

Cruisers setting out for the popular anchorage at Garden Key have a choice of a northerly route along Northwest Channel or the southerly Atlantic passage from Southwest Channel. Weather will often be the deciding factor for which route will be the most comfortable or fastest. Consult your guides and charts, but be sure to leave yourself enough time to reach the Dry

GARDEN KEY

FT JEFFERSON
ABAND LT HO